# ANCIENT CHINESE CIVILIZATION

This edition published in 2010 by:

The Rosen Publishing Group, Inc.
29 East 21st Street
New York, NY 10010

Cover design by Nelson Sa.

**Photo Credits:** Cover, pp. 1, 3 © www.istockphoto.com/Ilya Terentyev.

### Library of Congress Cataloging-in-Publication Data

Van Pelt, Todd.
Ancient Chinese civilization / Todd Van Pelt and Rupert Matthews ; illustrations by Francesca D'Ottavi.
  p. cm.—(Ancient civilizations and their myths and legends)
Includes bibliographical references and index.
ISBN-13: 978-1-4042-8035-9 (library binding)
1. China—Civilization—To 221 B.C.—Juvenile literature. 2. China—Civilization—221 B.C. to 960 A.D.—Juvenile literature. 3. China—Civilization—960–1644—Juvenile literature. 4. Mythology, Chinese—Juvenile literature. I. Matthews, Rupert. II. D'Ottavi, Francesca, ill. III. Title.
DS741.65.V36 2010
951—dc22

2009012362

*Manufactured in the United States of America*

Copyright © McRae Books, Florence, Italy.

# ANCIENT CIVILIZATIONS AND THEIR MYTHS AND LEGENDS

# ANCIENT CHINESE CIVILIZATION

TODD VAN PELT
AND RUPERT MATTHEWS

rosen publishing's
rosen
central
New York

# CONTENTS

# INTRODUCTION

Humans settled in China about 350,000 years ago, and the beginnings of Chinese civilization have been traced back to the Yellow River region. As the population of China grew, many small farming settlements joined together. Gradually, these villages developed into towns and cities, where power was held by ruling families. These families became known as dynasties, and some believe that the first dynasties were founded as early as 2200 BCE. Under the influence of different dynasties and religions, Chinese mythology and civilization developed into a rich mixture of ancient beliefs, new discoveries, and traditional learning. Many important inventions that are widely used today were first developed in ancient China, including the compass, the seismograph, and clockwork.

## HOW THIS BOOK WORKS

This book is divided into sections. Each section starts with a Chinese myth, strikingly illustrated on a black background. After each myth comes a double-page information section that looks at an aspect of Chinese culture and society, such as daily life, religion, or warfare.

The myth about the Eight Immortals, and their battles with the Dragon King, leads into a nonfiction section about Chinese religion.

*A myth is a story. It can be about the gods and their powers, the adventures of heroes, fabulous beasts, or strange places where mortal humans cannot go. In the ancient world, the Mesopotamians, Egyptians, and Greeks all told stories like these. The Chinese told myths too, and some of these have similar themes to those of other civilizations—for example stories about the creation of humanity and the world. Chinese mythology can be traced back almost 4,000 years, although many of the myths that survive today were recorded during the Han period. Although new beliefs developed, tales about the ancient Chinese deities remained popular.*

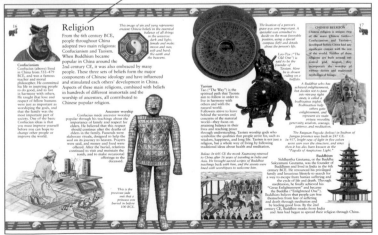

# PAN GU CREATES THE WORLD

At the very beginning, the universe was dark chaos in the shape of a round egg. It was not separated into heaven and earth, or day and night. The great giant, Pan Gu, slept curled up in the chaos. He lay there fast asleep for 18,000 years, all the time growing larger and larger. Then Pan Gu woke up. Because he was not satisfied with the chaos surrounding him, Pan Gu broke the eggshell open with an axe and a chisel.

As a result, the universe changed greatly. The light, clear matter rose and became heaven, and the thick, heavy matter sank and formed the earth. Pan Gu was worried that heaven and earth might join together, so he stood in the middle, holding up heaven with his head to keep it separate from the earth.

Every day during this period, heaven rose one zhang (equal to 11 feet 9 inches or 3.6 meters), earth grew one zhang, and Pan Gu also grew one zhang. This growth ceased after another 18,000 years. By this time Pan Gu was extremely tall, and the distance between heaven and earth was 90,000 li (equal to about 30,000 miles or 48,280 km). Pan Gu stood there alone, stopping heaven and earth from joining and collapsing back into chaos.

Many years passed. Pan Gu, who had been holding heaven up for a long time, felt very tired. Eventually, he lay down on the earth and died. His breath turned into winds and clouds; his voice became thunder; his left eye changed into the sun, and his right eye became the moon; his hair and beard transformed into stars; his arms and legs formed the four corners of the earth; and his body became the Five Sacred Mountains (the five most famous mountains in China).

Pan Gu's blood became flowing rivers; his veins turned into roads and paths; his muscles became fertile lands; his skin and fine hair changed into flourishing woods, grass, and beautiful flowers; his teeth and bones became metals and stones; his bone marrow became pearls and jades; and his sweat became rain and dew moistening the earth. And this is how a world that was suitable for human beings to live in was created.

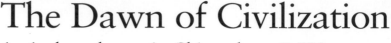

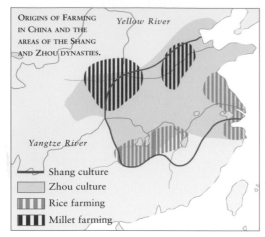

Yellow River

Yangtze River

Shang culture
Zhou culture
Rice farming
Millet farming

*Agriculture began in many different places: in the Yellow River basin, the Yangtze River basin, the southeast, the southwest, and in northern China.*

# The Dawn of Civilization

Agriculture began in China about 7,500 years ago. Farmers started cultivating rice along the lower areas of the Yangtze River, and this practice gradually spread inland and northward. Farther north, along the Yellow River, people began to grow millet. Loess (a deposit of fine, light-colored soil) made the land fertile for farming. Because of the civilization that was born as agriculture developed here, the Yellow River region became known as the cradle of the Chinese nation.

*These pictograph symbols (left), from the time of the Shang dynasty, show people transporting harvested crops. The same transport methods are still used in some parts of China today.*

## Yangshao culture

The Yangshao culture flourished on the plains of the Yellow River around 3200–2500 BCE. During this era, the people began to use hoes for plowing, and bows and arrows for hunting. Yangshao culture is also called "painted pottery culture" because much exquisite painted pottery from this period has been found. This red pottery was usually decorated with black designs of geometric shapes or images of animals.

*This bronze vessel shaped like an elephant (below) is covered in elaborate decorations. It was made during the Shang dynasty, between c. 1600 and c. 1050 BCE.*

*Yangshao pottery: the figure of a person (above) and a beautiful red painted vase (left). The geometric designs on this vase were typical of Yangshao pottery decoration.*

## The Bronze Age

The Xia dynasty, established in about the 21st century BCE, was the first Chinese dynasty. During this time people began to develop writing, metalworking, and also started to domesticate horses. In the 17th century BCE, King Tang overthrew the Xia dynasty and founded the Shang dynasty. People of the Shang dynasty built great cities, made beautiful bronze objects, and began making primitive porcelain. They bred cows, horses, sheep, and pigs, and also raised elephants. People believed in gods, and the kings always sought the gods' advice before beginning any activity.

The Chinese learned how to make pottery about 8,000 years ago. Banpo people made pottery by hand and fired it in a kiln (right). Flames were ignited in the fire chamber, and heat from the fire rose to the pottery chamber and fired the vessels. Most pottery made at this time was red or brown.

Pottery chamber

Fire chamber

*Black pottery, like this cup (left), was typical of the Lungshan culture of Shandong (c. 2010–1530 BCE). It is black because of the extremely high temperatures that the potters created in their kilns.*

## Banpo village

The Banpo people (5th–4th millennium BCE) lived in a Neolithic settlement in northern China. They grew crops (especially millet), fished, and gathered fruit and seeds, but they also raised animals such as pigs, sheep, and dogs. People in the village worked together and shared the food that they produced.

*Right: A reconstruction of a Banpo village. There was a large longhouse in the village center, where the villagers held meetings. There were many smaller clay houses around the big house, and these had earthen floors, thatched roofs supported by pillars, and fireplaces. A ditch surrounded the village, and outside this was a pottery-making area with several kilns.*

Thousands of years ago, people in China began to believe that the soul lived on after the body died, and they started to worship their ancestors, gods, and the forces of nature. Sacrifices of objects, animals, and sometimes even humans were believed to please the gods and ancestors. The ancient Chinese believed that heaven was round and the earth was square. Jade *pi* were circular disks with a small central hole, which symbolized the shape of heaven. They were probably sacrificed to gods and ghosts, and smaller ones might have been worn as decorative jewelry and used as a type of currency for trading.

*Above:* Pi *may have originally been used during worship of gods and ancestors. Larger ones came to symbolize wealth and high status.*

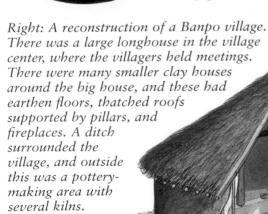

# NÜ WA CREATES THE HUMAN RACE

After the creation of heaven and earth, there were mountains and rivers, plains and trees, birds and animals, insects and fish—but there were no people. There was only the beautiful goddess Nü Wa.

Nü Wa felt very lonely, and one day while she was walking around on the earth, she wondered what she could add to the world to make it more lively. When she grew tired, she rested by the edge of a pond. She glanced into the water and saw her own reflection—then it struck her. She would make some living creatures that looked like her.

Nü Wa dug up some yellow earth next to the pond, and blended it with a little water. Using this mixture, she made a small creature that looked like her own image in the water. She put the little clay figure on the earth, and as it touched the soil, it came to life. Nü Wa named it Ren, meaning "human being."

Nü Wa was very satisfied with her work. She made one person after another. With all these little human beings around her, she no longer felt so lonely. Nü Wa hoped to make so many of them that they could spread all over the vast land. She worked until sunset and then started work again at dawn the following day. But Nü Wa grew very tired. Then she thought of a quicker way to work. She dipped a cane stem into the muddy water, and flicked it over the land. The little clay drops also became human beings.

Using this simple method, Nü Wa completed her task quickly. The humans she had shaped herself became the rich people, while those made from mud splashes became the poor. In order to continue the life of the human race, Nü Wa divided the people into men and women so they could produce their own children. In this way, the human race soon spread all over the world.

# Chinese Society

By the 3rd century BCE a ruling system based around the emperor and his officials was established. Important government decisions were made by these men in the imperial court. Local officials governed provincial areas, following the emperor's orders. From the Sui dynasty onward, special examinations were held to determine which men would become government officials. This system provided good career opportunities for intelligent, well-educated men, even if they were not from wealthy families.

## Civil servants

Government officials in China had either passed the official examinations or were from noble families. Low-level officials were often very poorly paid, while those in powerful positions could become extremely wealthy. Officials who worked closely with the emperor were highly respected, although their positions could be dangerous and unstable. There was an old saying: "Being around the emperor is like being around a tiger."

*This statue of a civil official (above) was made during the Tang dynasty, around 618–907 CE.*

*Guan Yu (left) was an historical warrior. A religious cult was built up around this legendary figure.*

## Soldiers

Soldiers in ancient China were either volunteers or men who had been forced into the army. Around the time of the Tang dynasty, a mercenary or paid army emerged. Life was hard for these men, who were separated from their families and risked their lives in battles. But some soldiers could become famous generals and improve their social positions. One common soldier even rose up through the ranks to ascend the throne as the first Song emperor.

## Dynasties

Chinese dynasties (ruling families) traditionally date back to the 27th century BCE. The Han dynasty held power by 206 BCE, and it unified China and built up the first Chinese Empire. But the Han dynasty lost power about 400 years later, and the empire crumbled. For a time, various rulers controlled different areas of the country, and smaller dynasties gained and lost power. Between 581 and 618 the Sui dynasty reunited the whole of China once more.

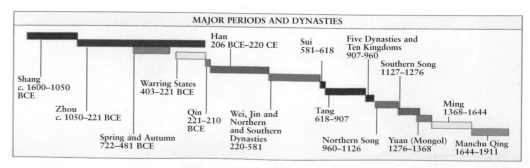

**MAJOR PERIODS AND DYNASTIES**

Shang c. 1600–1050 BCE
Zhou c. 1050–221 BCE
Spring and Autumn 722–481 BCE
Warring States 403–221 BCE
Qin 221–210 BCE
Han 206 BCE–220 CE
Wei, Jin and Northern and Southern Dynasties 220–581
Sui 581–618
Tang 618–907
Five Dynasties and Ten Kingdoms 907–960
Northern Song 960–1126
Southern Song 1127–1276
Yuan (Mongol) 1276–1368
Ming 1368–1644
Manchu Qing 1644–1911

This scholar (left), in a turban and a gown, was painted during the Song dynasty. Education and scholarship were always highly regarded in China.

In the painting of an emperor (below) the seriousness and responsibility of his position is shown by his dignified expression.

This painting (above) shows scholars sitting in an official examination. Although very difficult, these examinations brought many privileges to those who passed them successfully and became government officials. People continued to take them until 1905.

## Emperors

The color yellow was sacred to emperors, and all other people were forbidden to wear it. Many myths and common beliefs surrounded emperors; one of these was that they were descended from a dragon god and appointed by heaven. A large number of women lived in the palace as the emperor's favorites, and the one the emperor married became empress. Emperors' mothers were also given the title of empress. The emperor's decision about which son to name as his heir was often influenced by those around him.

## Peasants

Peasants made up the vast majority of the Chinese population, and their hard work was the basis of the agriculture that was so important to the country. But they lived very difficult lives and paid a large proportion of what they earned to landlords or in taxes. Peasants' standards of living were much lower than those of people in the cities, and their position did not improve much over thousands of years.

A dragon with five toes (left) was the official symbol of the emperor of China. The dragon symbolized goodness, strength, and wisdom.

This painting of a rice harvest (right) shows Chinese peasants separating grains of rice and carrying heavy loads.

# THE EIGHT IMMORTALS

The Eight Immortals were close friends and always spent a lot of time traveling, playing, and enjoying adventures together.

The Heavenly Empress, Hsi Wang–mu, threw a party once every 3,000 years, following the harvest of the peaches of immortality. After one of these very special parties, the Eight Immortals were too tired to ride home on the clouds, as they usually did, in case they fell off. So they decided to cross the seas instead.

They all floated safely on the waters, using magic objects as rafts; Chung–li rode on his feather fan, and Ti Guai Li rode on his iron cane. But the son of the Dragon King, who lived under the sea, became fascinated with the magic flute that Lan Ts'ai–ho was playing as she floated on her jade board. He sucked her down into the depths of the waters and stole her flute.

When the other seven Immortals realized that Lan was being held prisoner under the waves, they threatened to destroy the palace of the Dragon King unless she was freed immediately. But the Dragon King's son refused, and so a great battle began. In their anger, the Immortals lit huge fires, and the heat and flames burned the seas dry.

The friends found Lan and rescued her, but although they searched everywhere, they could not find her flute. Lan was filled with grief at losing her precious instrument, but the Immortals were running out of time as the Dragon King's warriors quickly poured water back into the sea basin in an effort to drown their attackers.

Just in time, the Immortals escaped to dry land. They were even more furious now, and used all their strength to topple an enormous mountain into the sea so that it wouldn't hold any more water. The battle raged on, until eventually the Dragon King's son was killed and the Immortals managed to recover Lan's flute, which he had been hiding. Then the Jade Emperor sent his Heavenly Guards down to make peace between the Dragon King and the Eight Immortals, and finally the fighting ceased.

# Religion

From the 6th century BCE, people throughout China adopted two main religions: Confucianism and Taoism. When Buddhism became popular in China around the 2nd century CE, it was also embraced by many people. These three sets of beliefs form the major components of Chinese ideology and have influenced and stimulated each others' development in China. Aspects of these main religions, combined with beliefs in hundreds of different immortals and the worship of ancestors, all contributed to Chinese popular religion.

*This image of yin and yang represents ancient Chinese beliefs in the essential balance of all things in the universe: dark and light; female and male; moon and sun; soft and hard; the earth and the heavens.*

**Confucianism**
Confucius (above) lived in China from 551–479 BCE, and was a famous teacher and moral philosopher. He committed his life to inspiring people to do good, and to live in harmony with others. He taught that love and respect of fellow humans were just as important as worshiping the gods, and that the family was the most important part of society. One of the basic Confucian ideas is that you must improve yourself before you can hope to change other people or improve the world.

**Ancestor worship**
Confucius made ancestor worship popular through his teachings about the importance of family and respect for elders. He believed that this respect should continue after the deaths of elders in the family. Funerals were elaborate rituals, designed to help the soul on its journey to heaven. Prayers were said, and money and food were offered. After the burial, relatives continued to visit and maintain the tomb, and to make occasional offerings to the deceased.

*This is the precious jade suit that a princess was buried in before 100 BCE.*

*The location of a person's grave was very important. A specialist was consulted to decide on the most favorable position, using a special compass (left) and details about the person's life.*

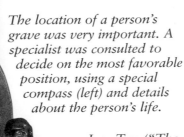

*Lao-Tzu ("The Old One") is said to be the founder of Taoism. Here he is shown riding on a buffalo.*

## CHINESE RELIGION

Chinese religion is unique; two of the main Chinese faiths—Confucianism and Taoism—developed before China had any significant contact with the rest of the world. Neither of these religions are built around one central god. Instead, they incorporate the worship of various deities and traditional mythological beings.

## Taoism

Tao ("The Way") is the spiritual path that Taoists aim to follow in order to live in harmony with others and with the natural world. Followers strive to leave behind the worries and concerns of the material world—they focus on attaining balance in their lives and reaching peace through understanding. Taoists worship gods who symbolize the qualities that people strive for, such as wisdom, happiness, and long life. Taoism is not just a religion, but a whole way of living by following traditional ideas about health and meditation.

*A Buddhist who has achieved enlightenment, but decides not to pass into nirvana right away, is called a bodhisattva (right). Bodhisattvas help others gain enlightenment, and represent six main virtues: morality, generosity, wisdom, courage, patience, and meditation.*

*The Ruiguan Pagoda (below) in Suzhou of Jiangsu province was built in 247 CE. In 937, bright rays of light in five colors were seen over the structure, and since then it has also been known as the "Pagoda of Auspicious Light."*

*Below: In 645 CE the monk Xuanzong returned to China after 16 years of traveling in India and Asia. He brought sacred scripts of Buddhist teachings back with him, and the streets were lined with worshipers to welcome him.*

## Buddhism

Siddhartha Gautama, or the Buddha Sakyamuni Gautama, was the founder of Buddhism and lived in India in the 6th century BCE. He renounced his privileged family and luxurious lifestyle to search for a way to escape from human suffering and the cycle of life and death. Through meditation, he finally achieved his "Great Enlightenment" and became the Buddha ("Enlightened One"). Buddhists believe that people can free themselves from fear of suffering and death through meditation and by leading good lives. By the 2nd century CE, Buddhist monks from India and Asia had begun to spread their religion through China.

# YAN DI, GOD OF AGRICULTURE AND MEDICINE

Yan Di (Lord Radiant) was a kind god. His head was like that of an ox, and he had a human body. As the number of people on the earth grew, there were no longer enough wild plants growing naturally to feed everybody. The people risked going hungry. When Yan Di saw this, he taught them how to cultivate the land and grow their own crops, to help them provide food for themselves.

As Yan Di was teaching the people, many grain seeds fell from the sky. Yan Di taught people how to sow these seeds in plowed fields. He made the sun to give enough light and heat for the crops to grow. The people finally had enough food to eat, and even some left over to store. They called Yan Di the Holy Farmer, or the God of Agriculture, to show their gratitude for his help.

Yan Di was also the God of Medicine. He had a magic red whip, and by using it to strike an herb plant, Yan Di could tell whether the plant was poisonous or not, and whether the plant's nature was basically hot or cold. In this way, he could find the right herbs to cure people's illnesses. But to find out exactly what effect certain herbs had, Yan Di tasted them himself. It was said that he was transparent, so if he tasted a poisonous herb, he could tell which part of his body was affected and use another herb to cure himself. Once, Yan Di was poisoned seventy times in just one day.

Eventually he died from eating a poisonous herb—some say it was called "Bowel-Breaking Weed," while others say it was the "Hundred–Legged Vermin" plant that killed him. But whichever plant it was, he sacrificed himself for the good of human beings—so they would know which plants were medicinal and which were poisonous.

In addition to teaching people how to farm and how to treat their illnesses, Yan Di also taught them how to make farming tools and pottery, and helped them create the calendar.

*This pottery goose is from the Western Han dynasty.*

*This vessel (below) was made in the shape of a boar. It is from the Shang dynasty, c.1600–c.1050 BCE.*

# Agriculture and Medicine

Agriculture was the basis of Chinese society. Many important changes were made to farming methods and techniques during the Han dynasty. New ideas about rotating crops to preserve the soil's fertility meant that farmers could produce more—and with more food available, the population grew rapidly. But the peasant farmers were still very poor and had to work hard to grow enough food to feed their families and pay taxes. However, the success of their crops was never guaranteed—droughts or floods could completely destroy everything they had grown. Plants were not only important as food, many were also used in medicines. Some traditional Chinese medicines are thousands of years old, and many are still used today.

## Farming developments

Better-designed plows became common during the Han dynasty, so farmers could prepare their fields for planting more easily. The state sponsored irrigation projects to help farmers water their crops. Ancient Chinese farmers were among the first in the world to fertilize their soil with animal manure, and they also invented the greenhouse.

*Below: A farmer using oxen to plow his fields for planting.*

*This knife (below) was used by farmers around 2000 BCE. It is one of the oldest agricultural tools to have ever been discovered.*

## Animals

The first Chinese farmers began raising animals, including sheep, goats, horses, chickens, dogs, and pigs. During the Han dynasty, farmers started to keep oxen to pull their plows—this meant that farmers were able to work larger areas of land. Donkeys were introduced to China and used to carry heavy loads. Ducks, chickens, geese, and pigs were all bred for their meat.

## Rice

Rice was not a main part of the Chinese diet until after about 1000 CE. It had been grown since neolithic times, but its popularity increased as settlement progressed in the south. The north was too cold and dry for rice to grow well. By the 13th century, a large amount of the hilly lower Yangtze area had been transformed into rice paddies, and the population had grown dramatically.

*Left: This vessel, shaped like a ram, was made in the Kingdom of Wu.*

*Right: This picture of a bull was drawn with ink and paint onto silk during the Tang period.*

## CHINESE MEDICINE

Traditional Chinese medicine is based on the belief that humans and their environment form a balanced whole, and that any disturbance to that balance can cause illness. Doctors use acupuncture, pressure points, massage, herbal medicines, and breathing therapy to balance the five basic types of energy in the body—these are represented by the elements believed to make up all matter: wood, fire, earth, metal, and water.

## Pressure points

The wrist (right) is an extremely important part of the body, according to Chinese medicine. Particular pressure points on the wrist are thought to relate to important parts of the body, such as the different organs. There are different pressure points all over the body.

*Traditional Chinese doctors believe there are 12 meridians or energy pathways in the body. One of these is shown on the right. Blood and air circulate through these channels. Yin and yang were thought to affect the movement of the blood vessels and to create the pulse.*

## Acupuncture

Acupuncture is an ancient Chinese medical technique developed to cure pain and disease and to improve general health. It was developed in China before 2500 BCE and involves inserting fine needles into certain points on the body depending on the problem. It is believed that this process can rebalance the *yin* and *yang* of the body and ensure that the *ch'i*, or vital life force, is able to flow freely. The popularity of acupuncture has spread throughout the world, and it is widely used today.

*The roots of the Shenan plant (left) were used to cure snake and insect bites.*

## Diagnosis

Information about the patient's pulse was very important to doctors trying to diagnose a condition. Doctors detected certain diseases by examining the strength, frequency, and rhythm of the pulse. In ancient China, men and women who were not related were not allowed to touch each other. Because of this, male doctors with a female patient had to tie a delicate silken thread around the woman's wrist in order to feel her pulse.

# WEAVING MAID AND COWHERD

Weaving Maid was a grandchild of the Emperor of Heaven. In heaven, she and her sisters wove beautiful colored clouds for the sky called "celestial garments." They changed color depending on what time of day and season it was.

At that time the Milky Way was the Silver River, and it lay in between heaven and earth. Cowherd and his old cow lived a lonely life on earth, on the other side of the Silver River. One day, the cow suddenly started to speak. She told Cowherd that the beautiful Weaving Maid was coming with other fairies to swim in the river. If Cowherd stole Weaving Maid's clothes while she was swimming, he could then marry her.

Cowherd went to the Silver River. Just as the cow said, Weaving Maid and her sisters came to the Milky Way, took off their silk gowns, and dived into the river. Cowherd grabbed Weaving Maid's clothes and refused to return them unless she agreed to marry him. Weaving Maid agreed. The two were married secretly and lived a very happy life together. Weaving Maid wove cloth and Cowherd farmed the land. They loved each other very much and had two children: one boy and one girl.

But one day the Emperor and Empress of Heaven found out that their granddaughter had married a mere mortal. They were so enraged that they snatched back Weaving Maid and locked her up. The Queen of Heaven shifted the Silver River up to heaven (where it was called the Milky Way) so that Cowherd could not cross over from earth.

The old cow told Cowherd that when she died he should wrap himself in her skin and fly to heaven. This he did, carrying the children. When they were almost there, the Queen of Heaven changed the Milky Way into a raging river. Cowherd could not cross it. He and his children used spoons to try and ladle out the water from the Milky Way, hoping to empty it so they could cross.

The Emperor of Heaven was so moved by their love for his granddaughter that he ordered magpies to form a bridge across the Milky Way—they still do this on every July 4 of the lunar calendar so that Weaving Maid and Cowherd can meet on the bridge once a year.

# Daily Life

Fashions in makeup, hairstyles, and clothing changed often among the upper classes, but styles among the common people changed very little for thousands of years. Poor people dressed in coarse hemp clothing. Most people lived in one-story homes in villages and shared community wells and granaries. Those living in the simplest houses did their cooking outside in the courtyard area. Wealthy people built wooden houses with several stories and had servants. They enjoyed a wide variety of foods, while the poor ate mainly vegetables, grains, and beans.

## Fashions

Women in ancient China decorated their faces using lead powder and different-colored substances. During the Sui dynasty, women used a spot of red or yellow color on their foreheads as decoration. Many women wore wigs so that they could create the elaborate coiled hairstyles that became fashionable during the Zhou dynasty.

*This pillow (left) from between 1115–1234 is made of glazed stoneware and painted with a hawk chasing a rabbit.*

*Above: This woman from the Middle Kingdom is holding a mirror and applying her makeup. She is decorating her forehead with the delicate shape of a tiny plum flower.*

*These special ceremonial court boots (below) were ornately decorated.*

*This tray (right) holds lacquer cups, plates, and chopsticks. They are decorated with a delicate cloud pattern. Items like these were used by upper-class people and were usually extremely expensive. Lacquer was made of tree sap and used to coat wooden or bamboo objects.*

*Tiny slippers like these (below) were worn by women with bound feet.*

## Tea

Tea became a popular drink during the Tang period. Before then it was used mainly as a medicine or as a drink for people who needed to stay awake. Tea became one of China's main crops as its popularity spread throughout the country.

## Footbinding

From the Song period onward, the feet of many young girls were tied tightly so they would stay small. It was believed that small feet made women attractive, but footbinding was very painful and made it impossible for the women to walk without help. Peasants never adopted this custom, as peasant women needed to work hard.

## HOUSES

Houses in ancient China were usually built of wood. They were a square shape, designed around a main room in the middle. Their families were very important to the ancient Chinese, and extended families often lived together. The most important family members lived in the main room, women lived in smaller interior rooms, and guests and male servants stayed in the outer rooms. It was considered extremely bad manners to enter the interior rooms of another person's home.

*This pottery model shows the kind of houses lived in during the Han dynasty. The small high windows kept hot summer sun out but let low winter sun in.*

*These two ceramic models show a man (probably a servant) washing dishes while kneeling (right) and a woman working at a dishwashing bench (left). The models were made in the Sui period.*

### Travel

Before the Shang period, simple vehicles had already appeared in China. During the Zhou dynasty the road system expanded, and by the Tang period networks of roads with cities at their centers had been formed. However, carriages were usually owned only by a privileged few; most people still traveled on foot.

### Fabrics

Around 6,000 years ago, the Chinese began raising silkworms to produce silk thread. They also made linen, and silk and linen became important fabrics for clothing. From the time of the late Song dynasty, cotton was another major material.

*This bronze model of a horse-drawn chariot was made around the 2nd century CE. Vehicles like this were used only by the upper classes.*

*Left: A dancing costume. The wide sleeves added to the grace and smoothness of the dancer's movements.*

# KING YAO

Yao was a very kind and wise king. He lived a plain and simple life, and his home was a thatched shack. Yao always tried to help his subjects, and they loved him with all their hearts.

One day, many favorable omens appeared around Yao's home. A phoenix, a holy bird, flew into his courtyard; all the horse-feed turned into rice; and lucky grasses started to grow in the backyard. It was believed that all these good things showed that the gods in heaven were pleased by Yao's kindness and wisdom.

Besides being an excellent king, Yao had also chosen very competent ministers to help him rule and make decisions. His judge, Gao Tao, had a magic, one-horned goat that could tell the guilty from the innocent. During courtroom trials, Gao Tao would ask this special goat to butt one of the suspects with his horn. The goat always butted the person who had done wrong. But if the person was innocent, the goat would refuse. Gao Tao therefore never made any mistakes in his trials. The goat was extremely useful and honest, so Gao Tao cared for it very well.

Yao had other ministers with unusual powers. The Minister of Music, Kui, had only one leg. He made music by imitating the sounds of nature, which calmed and soothed everybody who heard it. He beat stones together to create rhythm. His music was so beautiful and entrancing that all the birds and animals loved to dance to it.

Once, a strong old man who lived on pine seeds came to Yao. He brought Yao some of the seeds, but Yao was too busy to eat them. It was said that those who ate the pine seeds lived to be 200 or 300 years old.

# Art and Entertainment

Ancient Chinese art represented the lives and activities of many different Chinese people, not only the elite. Art forms included calligraphy (see p. 42), painting, storytelling, poetry, sculpture, music, and dancing. Early musical instruments included bamboo flutes, stone chimes, drums, pipes, and bells—they show us that music was part of even the oldest Chinese societies. From the late Zhou period onward, images of people hunting, making music, and waging war became common art subjects.

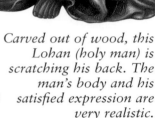

*Carved out of wood, this Lohan (holy man) is scratching his back. The man's body and his satisfied expression are very realistic.*

*This pottery sculpture (above) was made between 25–220 CE. It shows a storyteller joyfully performing with a drum.*

## Music

The oldest Chinese musical instruments ever found are thought to be over 7,000 years old. Until the time of the Tang dynasty, singing, dancing, and music developed together. After the Tang dynasty, until the collapse of Chinese feudal society, musical development focused on opera. Music was a main part of court life in ancient China—dancers and musicians entertained rulers and their visitors. The word for "music" was written with the same character as the word for "enjoyment."

*Above: These dancing figures (206 BCE–8 CE) are depicted holding cymbals. This bronze decoration would have been used to adorn a buckle.*

*Below: The illustration on this hanging silk scroll (from around 1190–1230 CE) shows a man listening to music played by women on their lutes.*

*This beautiful dragon sculpture (left) was made of gilt bronze and iron during the Tang dynasty. It shows the high level of skill among metalworkers at this time.*

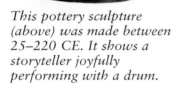

This image of beautiful women riding their horses decorated a silk handscroll (1049–1106 CE).

## Painting

The interior walls of palaces and temples were decorated with large and elaborate paintings, but not many of these have survived. Landscape painting was considered the most important style, and mountains were usually depicted, as they were thought to be sacred places. Ancient Chinese artists were painting landscapes long before Western artists thought of landscape as anything more than a background for their pictures.

Right: This tapestry is from 960–1279 CE. Huge mountains tower over the scene of a small thatched building on a clifftop.

Left: A board for playing a game of chance called liubo. The board is decorated with interweaving patterns of snakes. The game was sometimes used to try and predict the future, as well as being played for fun.

This glazed stoneware vase (left) is decorated with a dish-like top and a raised rib design. It was made during the Southern Song dynasty, around 1127–1279 CE.

## Games

The ancient Chinese invented many games for both entertainment and gambling. Some board games—such as "Go" and "Chinese checkers"—are still played, but most have now been forgotten. There were other games that were played during banquets. Many of these are still popular today.

This glazed horse statue was made during the Tang dynasty.

# THE BATTLE BETWEEN HUANG DI AND CHI YOU

Huang Di was the supreme god of the universe and the God of the Center. He had four faces that pointed toward north, south, east, and west, so he could see what was happening in all directions, and no one could trick him or act behind his back. Huang Di was also the ruler of the ghost world.

In order to strengthen his ruling position, Huang Di fought a war with the god of the south, Yan Di, and defeated him. Later, Chi You, a descendant of Yan Di, led a rebellion of the Miao people in the south, assisted by the ghosts of the mountains and forests.

They fought a fierce battle with Huang Di's army in Zhuolu. Chi You had about 80 brothers. Every one of them had an iron–hard head, four eyes, and six hands, and was extraordinarily ferocious and strong. They also possessed various magical powers. At first, fighting against such superhuman warriors, Huang Di and the gods and beasts suffered several defeats.

At one point, in the middle of a battle, Chi You blew a thick fog from his nostrils. Huang Di and his troops became trapped in the heavy clouds and could not escape. They became confused, not knowing which way to flee, and many of them were killed. The Queen of Winds took pity on them and invented the "compass cart," a vehicle decorated with an iron figure that always pointed south, so that Huang Di's troops could finally find their way out of the blinding fog.

Huang Di had a dragon named Dragon Ying, which could spread rainstorms. Huang Di asked Dragon Ying to attack Chi You, but before he could do this, Chi You ordered the Duke of Winds and the Master of Rains to create gales and storms to scatter Huang Di's troops.

Now Huang Di sought help from the Celestial Lady Ba, and she sent out fierce heat to dry up the storms. After many intense wars, Huang Di killed all of Chi You's brothers. Chi You himself was captured alive, imprisoned in chains, and then executed. His blood-stained shackles later became a maple forest, and his blood dyed the trees a flaming red color.

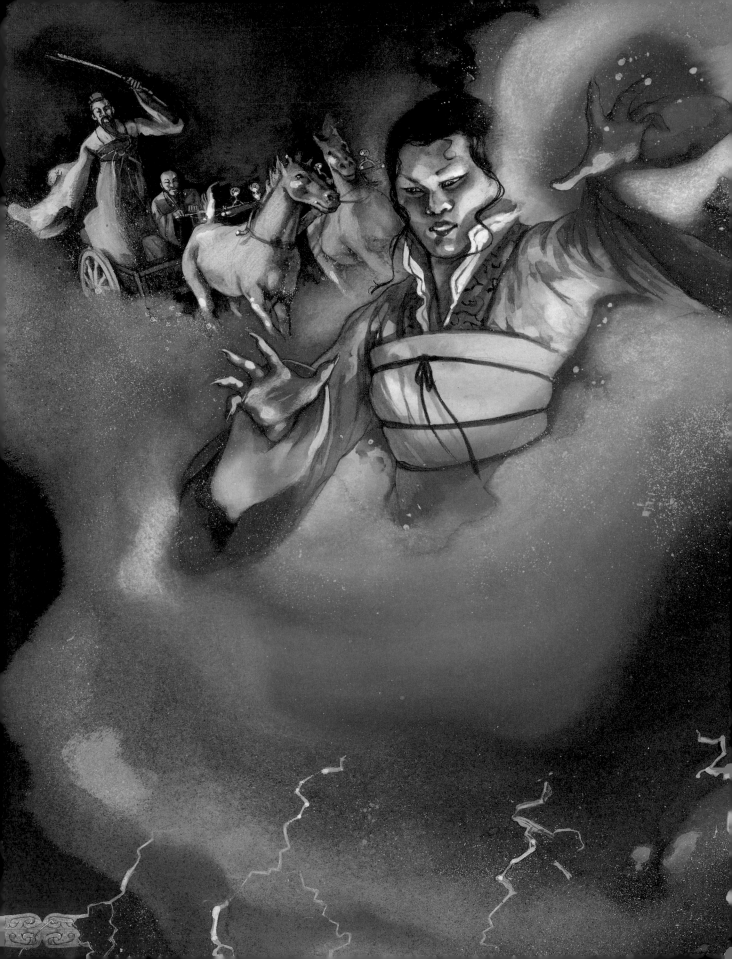

*Khubilai (Kubla) Khan (above) led the Mongols in their conquest of China.*

# War and Weapons

Wars and battles were common between different tribes and communities in ancient China. Cities were fortified with moats and walls from around the 21st century BCE, making them easier for their rulers and inhabitants to defend against attackers. Early weapons, made of bone, stone, and wood—and later bronze, iron, and steel—were used. By the 1100s weapons using gunpowder were beginning to appear. Methods for making weapons and armor continued to advance—new types of armor were needed to protect warriors as new and more deadly weapons were developed.

## Mongol conquest

In 1211 the Mongol leader Chinggis (Genghis) Khan began an attack on China. His troops were not skilled at warfare in densely populated areas, but they continued to advance, even after Chinggis's death. His grandson, Khubilai (Kubla) Khan, became the first outsider to rule over China when he established himself as emperor.

## Armor

During the Shang and Zhou periods, armor was made of thick, cotton-lined silk and iron. Later, bronze armor pieces had tiny holes so that they could be stitched to other armor made of leather or cloth. Iron armor—with the pieces strung together like overlapping scales—appeared during the Warring States period.

*Below: Part of the army of terra-cotta warriors buried in the First Emperor's funeral compound. The group includes figures of bowmen, archers, infantrymen, charioteers, and an armored rear guard, all arranged in military formation. They face east, because that is the direction the emperor's enemies had attacked from.*

*Above: This torso of a guardian king shows the ornate armor that may have been worn by the military elite during the Tang dynasty (618–907 CE).*

### THE TERRA-COTTA ARMY

More than 6,000 life-size terra-cotta soldiers and horses—together with war chariots and real weapons—were buried near the tomb of the First Emperor of Qin to defend him in the afterlife. The figures were originally painted with bright colors and were individually handfinished so that no two were exactly the same.

Warships (below) were often used during battles, especially in the south. Shipbuilding technology developed quickly, and huge ships with up to four levels appeared during the Han dynasty.

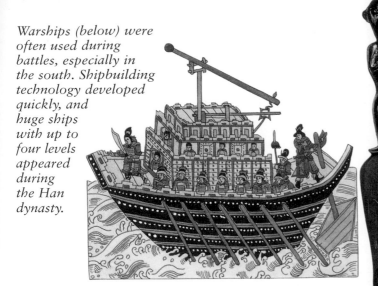

*Left: These swords were made between the 11th and the 4th centuries BCE. The hilt of the sword on the far left is decorated with a figure of a man and has a woman on the reverse. The other hilt is decorated with two tigers.*

*Below: Bronze arrowheads were used for crossbow arrows.*

*Below: Woodcuts from the Ming period show how deadly gunpowder could be when used in battles.*

## Gunpowder

The earliest written record of a recipe for gunpowder appeared in China in 1044, although the Chinese had been using it in fireworks and signals before the 10th century. By the 11th century, grenades, mines, and rockets containing gunpowder had been invented.

## Helmets

Helmets were made of iron or bronze. They were often decorated with feathers, or tassels, or with metal pieces cast to resemble animal faces.

*Above: These designs show the military uniforms worn by warriors during the Warring States period. The figures wear tunics that reach to the knee and protective caps and helmets.*

# THE TEN SUNS

Along time ago, there were ten suns. They were the sons of the Emperor of Heaven, and it was their duty to shine over the earth one at a time in an orderly fashion. But one day, during the period of King Yao's reign, these naughty children all appeared in the sky at the same time and danced around wildly.

The suns dried up all the crops in the soil, and people could hardly breathe in the heat. Even the witch who produced the rain died from too much sun. As well as creating serious drought, the severe heat also brought monsters out of the forests and swamps, and they attacked the people.

Yao, who loved his subjects as he loved his own sons, prayed to the Emperor of Heaven. The Emperor of Heaven sent one of his gods named Yi to help people on earth. He gave Yi a red bow and a bag of white arrows. Yi was a superb archer.

If he aimed at a target 100 times, he would hit it 100 times. He came to earth and shot dead all the fearsome monsters. Then Yi decided to get rid of those hateful suns and prepared ten arrows. At first he pretended to shoot at the suns, hoping that this might frighten them away. Yet they were not afraid. So Yi shot an arrow into the sky, and one sun exploded in a ball of fire. When it reached the earth, Yi saw that the sun had become a huge raven with three legs. After that, he shot down another eight suns.

Yao, who was watching beside Yi, thought that one sun would be useful to human beings. He asked his people to take away Yi's last arrow so that one sun was left in the sky. After that day, the remaining sun dared not misbehave. Every day it carries out its duty of providing light and heat for the world and disappears at night, allowing people to live, work, and sleep as normal.

It is said that the nine ravens fell into the ocean and formed a giant, scorching rock. Sea waters that crashed onto this rock evaporated. So even though water from all the rivers and streams flows into the sea, it never overflows.

# Inventions and Construction

*The wheelbarrow (below) has been used in China since as early as the 2nd century CE.*

Many marvelous inventions were used in ancient China long before they appeared in the West. Scientific and technological devices—such as the seismoscope, the compass, and clock mechanisms—appeared alongside inventions designed to improve the efficiency of farming, for example water pumps and wheelbarrows. Many impressive structures built for practical reasons by the ancient Chinese—like the Grand Canal and the Great Wall—still survive today. Among other contributions by the ancient Chinese to the development of the modern world are the "Four Big Inventions": papermaking, the compass, printing, and gunpowder.

*The square–pallet chain pump (above) was also called "the dragon backbone machine." Wooden pallets (to carry water) were fitted together in a chain, which circulated as operators pumped the pedals. In this way, water could be transported uphill from lower levels.*

*This painting (above), from the early Song period, shows the connections between grain production and distribution, water transport, and water–powered mills.*

*The mechanism that makes a clock keep time (the clock escapement) was invented in the 8th century. The huge clock tower illustrated on the left was built at Kaifeng in 1090. It stood about 30 feet (9 m) tall and operated using an escapement.*

*Below: A Chinese maritime compass. The compass had been adapted for use at sea by the 10th or 11th century.*

## Land, sea, and sky

Astronomy is an ancient science in China; charts of the sky have been found that are around 5,000 years old. These charts include star formations, comets, sunspots, and eclipses. Between the 1st and 3rd centuries CE, the Chinese discovered that shaped lodestones and magnetized needles pointed north or south, and needles were used for navigation from this time onwards.

*This observation of sunspots (right) was painted in 1425 by the Ming emperor Hongxi. He also painted other depictions of the atmosphere around the sun.*

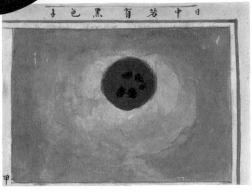

*In 132 CE, Zhang Heng (astronomer and mathematician) invented this earthquake weathercock. Seismoscopes like this were not invented in other parts of the world until 1703, when one was made in France.*

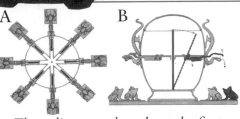

*These diagrams show how the first seismoscope worked. A: Earth tremors shifted a heavy metal bar inside. B: A metal ball was released from the jaws of the dragon that pointed in the direction of the tremor. The ball then dropped noisily into the frog's open mouth below.*

## The Grand Canal

ROUTE OF THE SUI AND TANG GRAND CANAL

Beijing

Luoyang

Hangzhou

⊔⊔⊔ GRAND CANAL

The Grand Canal (diagram left) links the north and south of China, and is the longest human-made waterway in the world. It stretches over a distance of about 1,085 miles (1,747 km). The oldest section of the canal may have been constructed as early as the 4th century BCE.

*The Great Wall of China is the only human-made structure on earth that can been seen from the moon.*

## The Great Wall

The First Emperor of Qin laid the foundations of the Great Wall at the end of the Warring States period when he had succeeded in unifying China. Later governments continued work on the wall, as Chinese control extended westward. The wall was a military boundary, and is dotted with fortresses and watchtowers. It also separated the nomads of the north from the southern farming settlements.

# THE FIRST SILKWORM

Once upon a time, there was a man who left his home to travel to a faraway place, leaving behind his little daughter and his horse. The girl took good care of the horse, but she felt very lonely because her father had been away for a long time.

One day, the girl spoke jokingly to the horse: "If you could bring my father home, I would marry you." When it heard her words, the horse wrenched itself free from its tether and ran off to find her father. After several days he found him and neighed sadly, looking in the direction of home.

The father immediately imagined that something terrible had happened to the girl. He quickly mounted the horse to return to his daughter, and they were joyfully reunited. Of course, he did not know why the horse had come for him. He simply thought that the animal was clever and loyal.

So the man offered his horse good feed and cared for him well. But the horse did not want to eat anything, and every time he saw the little girl, he jumped up and down and neighed. The father thought that this was rather strange. When he asked his daughter about the horse's behavior, she confessed the promise she had made to the horse.

The father was angry and said it was impossible that a human being should marry an animal. With his bow and arrow he shot the horse dead. He laid the skin on the ground outside in the sun to dry. One day, when the father was not at home, his daughter and her friends were playing together near the horsehide. Suddenly, the hide jumped up from the ground, wrapped itself tightly around the girl, and disappeared with her. A few days later, her father found her in a mulberry tree. The girl wrapped in the horsehide had become a silkworm, spinning silk in the tree. This is the origin of the silkworm.

# Trade

China has been trading with, and influencing, other parts of the world for thousands of years. Chinese silk was being sold in India by about the 4th century BCE. Trade was important not only for material reasons, but also because the ideas of different cultures came into contact as goods were exchanged. Japan, for example, was influenced by many aspects of Chinese culture, including religion and writing. Chinese traders transported goods overland, through Central Asia to the Mediterranean, and also carried goods to the West over the seas.

*Zheng He was an admiral who led naval expeditions. He returned from Africa in 1414 with a giraffe.*

*These gilded bronze leopards (below) may have been used as weights to measure goods and money.*

### Weights and measures

Before China was united under the First Emperor of Qin, every state had its own systems of weights and measures. This made trading between the states very difficult.

*This porcelain table screen (above) is inscribed in Arabic with a chapter from the Koran. Such items were made in China either for Muslims living at the imperial court or for export to Muslim countries.*

*This map (right) shows some of the routes taken by traders and travelers to and from China.*

TRADE ROUTES
Fu-Hsien 399–414 CE
Hsūan-Tsang 629–645 CE

PERSIA  ASIA
ARABIA  INDIA
ARABIAN SEA
AFRICA  BAY OF BENGAL
INDIAN OCEAN  SOUTH CHINA SEA

### Silk

In classical times, the Greeks and Romans called the Chinese "Seres," meaning "silk people." Sericulture (the production of silk) has been practiced in China for thousands of years, perhaps since as long ago as 7000 BCE. The Silk Road was an ancient route that traders traveled to carry goods, particularly silk, from China to the West. From the West, China imported items such as wool and gold. The Silk Road began at Sian, and stretched 4,000 miles (6,400 km) to the shores of the Mediterranean.

*Right: Camels were used as pack animals to transport goods such as cloth across long distances.*

*Left: Women pressing newly woven silk with an iron. The silk is then wound tightly to keep it flat.*

## CURRENCY

A: Cowrie shells had long been used in ancient China as a form of currency that was exchanged for goods. The other coins shown here (left) were in circulation around the 5th century CE. B: The dao, in the shape of a knife, was used in the northeast. C: Bu coins, shaped like a spade, were common in the northwest. D: Bronze Chinese coins with the square hole were made and used for about 2,500 years, in roughly the same shape and size. They were eventually used all over the country after China was unified as one empire.

B

D

A

C

*Paper money was first printed in the 11th century. It was much easier to carry notes of paper than the weight of all the coins they represented.*

### Sea transport

As the magnetic compass came into use and navigation techniques developed, ships were increasingly used to transport trade goods over the seas. Many coastal settlements became important commercial ports.

*Chinese trading ships traveled to many parts of the world, including South Asia, the Red Sea, and the Persian Gulf.*

### Porcelain

Chinese potters were making earthenware vessels and statues as early as neolithic times. During the Stone Age, stoneware developed, and the technique of glazing began in China. Fine white porcelain, which became known abroad as "china," first appeared during the Tang dynasty.

*Oxen were often used as pack animals, and ox carts were used to transport goods and people. This ceramic model was made in Taiyuan around the middle of the 6th century.*

*This precious porcelain "moon flask" (right) is decorated in cobalt blue with the figure of a dragon among lotuses. It was made between 1403–1424, during the Ming dynasty.*

# Education, Writing, and Literature

The tradition of Chinese literature is more than 3,000 years old— making it one of the oldest literary heritages in the world. It began with poetry; other forms of literature then developed, including prose, short stories, novels, drama, and history. The main kinds of poetry were originally sung to music. Calligraphy is one of the ways that literature, especially poetry, was recorded; this beautiful form of handwriting takes many years to perfect, and the individual characters are regarded as art forms in themselves. Traditional education was based around learning to write the thousands of Chinese characters and the study of ancient texts and ideas.

*Oracle bones (left) are etched with the earliest form of Chinese writing yet discovered.*

*This illustration shows the correct way to hold a calligraphy brush.*

## Oracle bones

The oldest examples of Chinese writing are engraved on animal bones, or tortoise shells, dating from the 18th century BCE. During ceremonies, the bones or shells were heated as diviners asked questions of the spirit ancestors. Cracks that appeared in the bones were interpreted as the spirits' answers. Using symbols, the questions and answers were inscribed onto the bones with sharp metal instruments. Sometimes, later events believed to be related to the predictions were also recorded on the bones.

## Papermaking

Early samples of Chinese paper (made of rags, hemp, and other fibers) have been dated back to the 2nd century BCE. After 105 CE, papermakers began to use the barks of certain plants to make finer-quality paper. Later, paper was also made of rice straws, wheat straws, and bamboo. Arabs took the secret of papermaking from China to Europe in the 8th century.

*Yong (above), meaning eternity, is a calligraphy character that contains the 8 basic strokes.*

## Calligraphy

Calligraphy is a form of Chinese writing that developed into an art form. A piece of calligraphy would be judged on the expressiveness of the work and also on the technique. Good calligraphy was important for passing the imperial examinations. It was believed that personal integrity was demonstrated by straight, clear handwriting—in other words, good calligraphy meant an admirable personality.

*To make paper, plant fibers were first put in a basin or shallow box to soak.*

*The pulp was then lifted out, smoothed onto a flat grid, and dried.*

*After drying, the pulp solidified into a flat sheet of paper.*

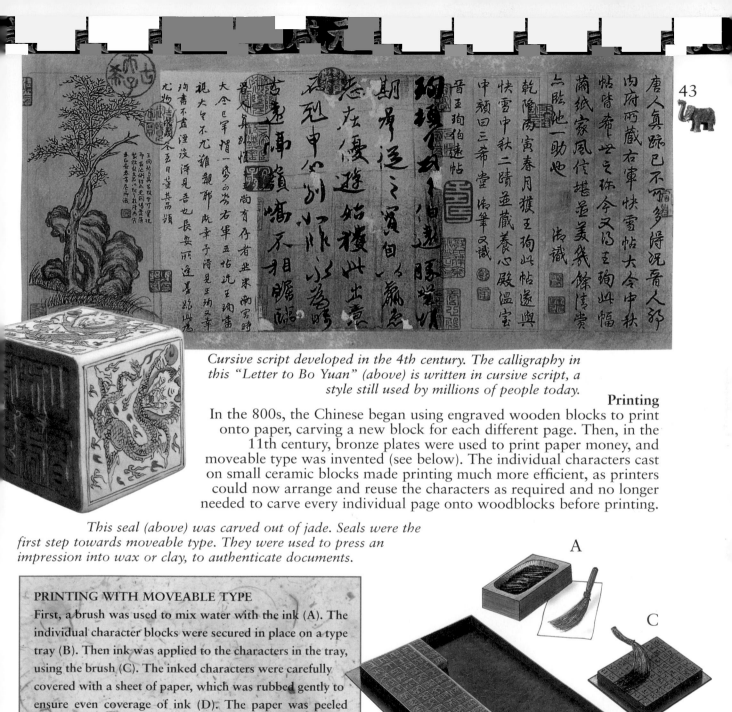

*Cursive script developed in the 4th century. The calligraphy in this "Letter to Bo Yuan" (above) is written in cursive script, a style still used by millions of people today.*

## Printing

In the 800s, the Chinese began using engraved wooden blocks to print onto paper, carving a new block for each different page. Then, in the 11th century, bronze plates were used to print paper money, and moveable type was invented (see below). The individual characters cast on small ceramic blocks made printing much more efficient, as printers could now arrange and reuse the characters as required and no longer needed to carve every individual page onto woodblocks before printing.

*This seal (above) was carved out of jade. Seals were the first step towards moveable type. They were used to press an impression into wax or clay, to authenticate documents.*

### PRINTING WITH MOVEABLE TYPE

First, a brush was used to mix water with the ink (A). The individual character blocks were secured in place on a type tray (B). Then ink was applied to the characters in the tray, using the brush (C). The inked characters were carefully covered with a sheet of paper, which was rubbed gently to ensure even coverage of ink (D). The paper was peeled away (E) with the characters printed on it.

## Education

Private schools appeared during the Spring and Autumn periods (c. 722–481 BCE). Confucius (551–479 BCE) is known as the first teacher in China; he believed that education should be made available to all men, and he had many students. Until modern times, Chinese education was strongly based around historical and philosophical texts from the late Zhou period.

# GLOSSARY

**ancestor** Any person from whom one is descended; a forebear.

**calligraphy** Beautiful handwriting; handwriting as art.

**civil servant** Someone employed in government administration; any government service in which a position is secured through competitive public examination.

**cultivate** To prepare and use soil and land for growing crops; to grow plants or crops from seeds, bulbs, or shoots.

**diviner** Someone who prophesies or guesses with supernatural aids or assistance.

**domesticate** To tame wild animals or plants and use them for human purposes.

**dynasty** A succession of rulers who are members of the same family.

**elaborate** Worked out carefully; developed in great detail; highly wrought or ornamented; painstaking.

**enlightenment** The state of having truth revealed to one; to be free of ignorance, prejudice, and superstition.

**feudal** A social and political system in which land was worked by a servant or slave class and landowners owed allegiance and military service to the region's ruler or lord.

**granary** A building for storing threshed grain.

**hemp** A plant grown for the tough fiber in its stem, which can be used to make such things as rope, sailcloth, and clothing.

**ideology** The doctrines, opinions, or way of thinking of an individual, class, church, organization, political party, or government; the body of ideas on which a particular political, economic, or social system is based.

**imperial** Relating to empire and the rule of an empire and its emperor.

**lodestone** A strongly magnetic variety of the mineral magnetite.

**meditation** Deep, continued thought; deep reflection on sacred or spiritual matters as a devotional act.

**millet** A cereal grass used for food.

**monk** A man who retires from the world and lives in a state of solitary self-denial for religious reasons; a man who joins a religious order living in retirement and often bound by vows of poverty and obedience.

**nomad** Someone having no permanent home who moves about constantly in search of food and pasture.

**philosopher** A person who studies and is accomplished in the search for wisdom or knowledge, including the nature of the universe, being, and reality.

**primitive** Existing in the beginning or earliest time; ancient; crude; simple.

**ritual** A set form of rites, often religious in nature; the observance of these set forms of rites, such as in public worship.

Asia Society
725 Park Avenue
New York, NY 10021
(212) 288-6400
Web site: http://www.asiasociety.org
Asia Society is the leading global
organization working to strengthen
relationships and promote understanding
among the people, leaders, and
institutions of Asia and the United
States. Founded in 1956, Asia Society
is a nonpartisan, nonprofit educational
institution with offices in Hong Kong,
Houston, Seoul, Los Angeles, Manila,
Melbourne, Mumbai, New York,
San Francisco, Shanghai, and
Washington, D.C.

Center for Chinese Studies (CCS)
University of California, Berkeley
2223 Fulton Street, Room 505
Berkeley, CA 94720-2328
The CCS is the largest and most active
research unit within the Institute of East
Asian Studies (IEAS). The CCS covers all
areas of Chinese studies with an energetic
program of extracurricular activities. In
addition to lectures and colloquia, CCS
convenes large-scale symposia and
smaller conferences on key issues,
inviting national and international
specialists to confer and share their
research. Research sponsored by the
center now focuses not only on the
People's Republic of China but on the
Chinese societies of Taiwan, Hong Kong,
and Southeast Asia as well.

China National Tourist Office (CNTO)
370 Lexington Avenue, #912
New York, NY 10017
(800) 760-8218
Web site: http://www.cnto.org
CNTO is an overseas office of the China
National Tourism Administration
(CNTA), whose headquarter is in
Beijing. CNTA has fifteen overseas
tourist offices around the world,
including three in North America: New
York, Los Angeles, and Toronto. CNTA
is the governmental tourism organization
directly regulated by the State Council,
whose responsibility is to promote and
administer China's tourism industry.

Department of Asian Studies
University of British Columbia
Asian Centre
1871 West Mall
Vancouver, BC V6T-1Z2
(604) 822-0019
Web site: http://www.asia.ubc.ca
This is the leading program in Asian
studies in Canada and among the best
programs in North America.

Freer Gallery of Art/Arthur M.
Sackler Gallery
Smithsonian Institution
P.O. Box 37012, MRC 707
Washington, DC 20013-7012
(202) 633-1000
Web site: http://www.asia.si.edu
The Freer Gallery houses a world-
renowned collection of art from China,

Japan, Korea, South and Southeast Asia, and the Near East. Visitor favorites include Chinese paintings, Japanese folding screens, Korean ceramics, Indian and Persian manuscripts, and Buddhist sculpture. The Sackler Gallery features early Chinese bronzes and jades; Chinese paintings and lacquerware; ancient Near Eastern ceramics and metalware; sculpture from South and Southeast Asia; Islamic book arts from the eleventh to the nineteenth century; nineteenth- and twentieth-century Japanese prints and contemporary porcelain; Indian, Chinese, Japanese, and Korean paintings; arts of village India; contemporary Chinese ceramics; and photography.

The Rubin Museum of ART (RMA)
150 West 17th Street
New York, NY 10011
(212) 620-5000
Web site: http://www.rmanyc.org/index.php
The RMA is home to a comprehensive collection of art from the Himalayas and surrounding regions. Through changing exhibitions and an array of engaging public programs, the RMA offers opportunities to explore the artistic legacy of the Himalayan region and to appreciate its place in the context of world cultures. The RMA collection consists of paintings, sculptures, and textiles. Although works of art range in date over two millennia, most reflect major periods and schools of Himalayan art from the twelfth century onward.

UCLA Center for Chinese Studies
11381 Bunche Hall
Los Angeles, CA 90095-1487
(310) 825-8683
Web site: http://www.international. ucla.edu/china
Founded in 1986, the UCLA Center for Chinese Studies has achieved distinction and an international reputation for excellence under the aegis of UCLA's International Institute. The program offers unusual strength in a wide variety of disciplines and fields, including anthropology, archaeology, art history, geography, history, law, linguistics, literary studies, medicine, political science, and sociology.

## Web Sites

Due to the changing nature of Internet links, Rosen Publishing has developed an online list of Web sites related to the subject of this book. This site is updated regularly. Please use this link to access this list:

http://www.rosenlinks.com/anc/chinese

# FOR FURTHER READING

Challen, Paul. *Life in Ancient China* (Peoples of the Ancient World). New York, NY: Crabtree Publishing Co., 2004.

Fu, Shelley. *Treasury of Ancient Chinese Folk Tales: Beloved Myths and Legends from the Middle Kingdom*. North Clarendon, VT: Tuttle Publishing, 2008.

Greenblatt, Miriam. *Han Wu Di and Ancient China* (Rulers and Their Times). New York, NY: Benchmark Books, 2005.

Kalman, Bobbie. *China: The Land* (Lands, Peoples, and Cultures). New York, NY: Crabtree Publishing Co., 2008.

Knox, Barbara. *Forbidden City: China's Imperial Palace* (Castles, Palaces, and Tombs). New York, NY: Bearport Publishing, 2006.

Opik, E. J., and Laura Buller. *Ancient China* (DK Eyewitness Books). New York, NY: DK Children, 2005.

Primary Source, Inc. *The Enduring Legacy of Ancient China*. Boston, MA: Cheng & Tsui, 2006.

Roberts, Jeremy. *Chinese Mythology A to Z* (Mythology A to Z). New York, NY: Facts on File, 2004.

Schomp, Virginia. *The Ancient Chinese* (People of the Ancient World). New York, NY: Children's Press, 2005.

Sebag-Montefiore, Hugh. *China* (DK Eyewitness Books). New York, NY: DK Children, 2007.

Shone, Rob. *Chinese Myths* (Graphic Mythology). New York, NY: The Rosen Publishing Group, 2006.

Wilkinson, Philip. *Chinese Myth: A Treasury of Legends, Art, and History* (The World of Mythology). Armonk, NY: Sharpe Focus, 2007.

# INDEX